THE 10

Greatest
Sports Showdowns

Glen Downey

Series Editor
Jeffrey D. Wilhelm

Much thought, debate, and research went into choosing and ranking the 10 items in each book in this series. We realize that everyone has his or her own opinion of what is most significant, revolutionary, amazing, deadly, and so on. As you read, you may agree with our choices, or you may be surprised — and that's the way it should be!

Franklin Watts®
an imprint of
SCHOLASTIC
www.scholastic.com/librarypublishing

A Rubicon book published in association with Scholastic Inc.

Ru'bìcon © 2008 Rubicon Publishing Inc.
www.rubiconpublishing.com

 is a trademark of The 10 Books

Associate Publishers: Kim Koh, Miriam Bardswich
Project Editor: Amy Land
Editor: Jessica Calleja
Creative Director: Jennifer Drew
Project Manager/Designer: Jeanette MacLean
Graphic Designer: Doug Baines

The publisher gratefully acknowledges the following for permission to reprint copyrighted material in this book.

Every reasonable effort has been made to trace the owners of copyrighted material and to make due acknowledgment. Any errors or omissions drawn to our attention will be gladly rectified in future editions.

"He Guaranteed It" (excerpt) by Ray Didinger. Reprinted with permission from the Super Bowl XXXII Official Game Program, NFL Publishing. All Rights Reserved.

Cover: Muhammad Ali (right) punches Joe Frazier (left) in the head during the seventh round of Thrilla in Manila in 1975–© Bettmann/CORBIS

Library and Archives Canada Cataloguing in Publication

Downey, Glen R., 1969–
    The 10 greatest sports showdowns / Glen Downey.

Includes index.
ISBN 978-1-55448-535-2

    1. Readers (Elementary). 2. Readers—Sports.
I. Title. II. Title: Ten greatest sports showdowns.

PE1117.D6933 2007a   428.6   C2007-906702-6

1 2 3 4 5 6 7 8 9 10   10   17 16 15 14 13 12 11 10 09 08

Printed in Singapore

Contents

BATTLE OF THE BEST

For some people, sports are just games that they don't take too seriously. But for others, winning is everything. These athletes are the elite competitors who have the determination, focus, and drive to be the best. They would do anything to make it to the top. It's all about the glory and the trophy.

Rivalries, clashes, and fierce competitions in a sport are not uncommon. Just talk to some sports fans and you will surely hear stories of memorable sports showdowns. Some of these may be a single, much-hyped match; others an intense rivalry that lasts for years.

Like all sports fans, we have our own list of what we think are the 10 greatest sports showdowns of all time. We selected and ranked them using these criteria: they involved huge stakes with pride, glory, and prizes on the line; they created high levels of excitement; they involved well-known competitors, often with long-standing rivalries; and they had a lasting impact, both inside and outside the sport.

As you read, you might be surprised by some of our choices. Decide for yourself:

What is the greatest sports showdown?

Canadian figure skater Brian Orser (left), American Brian Boitano (center), and Ukrainian Viktor Petrenko (right), smile on the podium following the men's competition at the 1998 Olympic Winter Games held in Calgary, Alberta.

ITANO

SPORT: Olympic Men's Figure Skating

WHEN: February 20, 1988, Calgary, Alberta

THE SHOWDOWN: Canadian Brian Orser and American Brian Boitano are both talented skaters who are their country's best hope for gold.

There was no question what the main event of the 1988 Winter Olympics was going to be — a showdown dubbed "The Battle of the Brians."

Brian Orser was a Canadian figure skating champion who was known for his artistic flair on the ice. American Brian Boitano was also a well-known skating star who was technically skilled and precise, but short on artistry. The two had been competing for years. They had faced off in international skating tournaments several times before. Each had victories to show for it. Orser took the Olympic silver medal in 1984, with Boitano finishing fifth. At the 1987 World Championships, Boitano came in second to Orser's championship performance.

Even in Calgary, Orser and Boitano were neck and neck. Each skater had already placed first in earlier programs. They were so close that whoever won the long program would be crowned Olympic champion. All of their hard work came down to one performance on one night. All each skater had to do was concentrate on proving to the judges that he deserved to win.

ORSER VS. BOITANO

PLAYERS

Brian Orser was a man on a mission. He was proud of his silver medal from the 1984 Olympics, but wanted more. In that competition he was beaten by Scott Hamilton of the United States, even though he had won both the long and short programs. Brian Boitano also had something to prove. After losing to Orser in the 1987 World Championships, he was determined to jazz up his performances by adding new jumps.

PLAY-BY-PLAY

Orser and Boitano were well matched in many ways. Both skaters were their country's national champions and favorites for the gold. Leading up to the competition, they faced constant attention from the media. But they overcame the pressure and gave exceptional performances. Though not as artistically gifted as Orser, Boitano gave a near-perfect performance. Orser went next and wobbled on one landing. With the world holding its breath, Boitano took gold.

IMPACT

The Battle of the Brians is considered one of the most memorable competitions in figure skating history. It stands for the best that the Olympics has to offer. While there was a media frenzy over the so-called battle, the two skaters were friendly off the ice. Figure skating has seen a number of scandals over the years, but the duel between Orser and Boitano was a situation where the competitors determined the outcome by skating their best.

Canadian figure skater Brian Orser performs his free program during the men's competition at the 1988 Olympic Winter Games.

How do you think the pressure from an entire country to perform well would have affected both Orser and Boitano leading up to the Olympic Games?

The Expert Says...

" There was a lot of pressure at the time ... Wherever I went people shouted 'Go for the gold!' I was even approached at the grocery store ... "

— Brian Orser

10

9   8   7   6

CLOSE CALL

THIS REPORT EXPLAINS JUST HOW CLOSE THIS COMPETITION REALLY WAS.

Those who watched The Battle of the Brians knew they were witnessing something special. Going into the free skating part of the men's competition, Boitano and Orser were tied for first place. The difference between their scores was so small that the skater who won the long program would win the title.

The judging could not have been closer. Four judges voted for Orser, three voted for Boitano, and two scored it a tie. The judges who gave Orser and Boitano equal marks decided that the score for technical merit should be the tiebreaker. As both judges awarded Boitano higher marks for technical merit, he ended up winning 5–4.

THE OFFICIAL SCORECARDS

BOITANO	FRG	USA	DEN	URS	SUI	JPN	GDR	CAN	TCH
TECHNICAL MERIT	5.8	5.9	5.9	5.9	5.9	5.8	5.8	5.8	5.9
ARTISTIC IMPRESSION	5.8	5.9	5.7	5.8	5.8	5.9	5.8	5.8	5.9
PLACEMENT	2	1	1	1	1	1	2	2	2

ORSER	FRG	USA	DEN	URS	SUI	JPN	GDR	CAN	TCH
TECHNICAL MERIT	5.8	5.8	5.8	5.8	5.8	5.8	5.8	5.8	5.9
ARTISTIC IMPRESSION	5.9	5.9	5.8	5.8	5.9	5.8	5.9	5.9	6.0
PLACEMENT	1	2	2	2	2	2	1	1	1

 What do you think is more important when judging figure skating — technical merit or artistic impression? Explain why.

Quick Fact

The two Brians dueled again at the 1988 World Championships in Budapest. Orser placed second once again behind Boitano. Shortly after this competition, Orser retired from amateur skating and went pro.

Take Note

The Battle of the Brians has been celebrated by some critics as the greatest men's figure skating competition in history. The showdown between Orser and Boitano had unbelievable hype, was an amazing competition, and left a legacy of excellence that went beyond the sport. That is why it kicks off our list at #10.

- What does it say about the two men's competitive spirit that they were friendly both on and off the ice even though each faced such intense pressure to win? How would you handle a situation like this?

5   4   3   2   1

Joan Benoit (center) receives the gold medal after winning the women's marathon at the 1984 Summer Olympic Games in Los Angeles, California. Rival Grete Waitz (left) receives silver.

SPORT: 42 km [26 mi.] Women's Olympic Marathon

WHEN: August 5, 1984, Los Angeles, California

THE SHOWDOWN: Joan Benoit, two-time Boston Marathon winner, goes up against New York City Marathon champ and living legend Grete Waitz.

The marathon is sport's ultimate test of mental strength and endurance. Athletes run over a gruelling 42 kilometers [26 miles] — that's about 105 laps around a regular 400-meter [437 yards] track. Before 1984, there was no women's running event longer than 1,500 meters [1,640 yards] in the Olympics. The women's marathon race was finally added to the 23rd Olympic Games in Los Angeles, California. It was to be a historic showdown between two top runners.

Joan Benoit was a gutsy marathoner from the United States. She won the 1984 Olympic trials (in which athletes compete for the chance to represent their country) only 17 days after having knee surgery. On the big day, she approached the starting line of the race determined to win. Grete Waitz was a Norwegian superstar who was already one of the finest women's distance runners of the 20th century. She had beaten Benoit in 10 of the last 11 races in which they competed and wanted to maintain her winning streak. The pressure to win was front and centre in the minds of both athletes.

BENOIT VS. WAITZ

PLAYERS

Joan Benoit and Grete Waitz were both standout marathoners and future Hall of Famers. By 1984, Benoit had already won the famous Boston Marathon twice. Waitz was also a recognized runner — at the time she was already a world record holder and a five-time New York City Marathon winner. Even though it seemed that Waitz had the edge going into this race, both runners were seen as possible gold medallists.

PLAY-BY-PLAY

At the 1984 Olympics in Los Angeles, many gifted athletes competed in the women's marathon. Sports announcers and fans knew August 5, 1984 was going to be an exciting day. Just 14 minutes into the race, Benoit took the lead. Wearing her white painter's cap, she steadily pulled ahead of the pack. Waitz couldn't reel her back in and neither could anyone else. Benoit ended up taking gold and finished the race with a time of 2:24:52. This was more than a minute faster than her rival.

? What characteristics do you think a marathoner must have?

Joan Benoit is the front-runner breaking away from the pack. Grete Waitz (289) is seen second from left.

Quick Fact

This race is also remembered for Gabrielle Andersen-Scheiss, a Swiss competitor who had heat exhaustion. She staggered into the stadium for her final lap with a stiff right leg and her left arm hanging limply by her side. She was determined to finish, taking five minutes and 44 seconds to complete the lap. She fell into the arms of waiting medics when she reached the finish line.

IMPACT

The image of Benoit with her white cap surging into the lead, then speeding up and never for a moment looking like she was going to stop, inspired female athletes around the world. With so many strong runners, this race proved once and for all that women could run a marathon. Benoit became a role model for a new generation of athletes.

10   9   8   7   6

Racing Toward Equality

This timeline runs through some standout moments for female athletes …

1922

The Women's World Games (also called the Women's Olympics) is held in Paris. Lucie Bréard wins the 1,000-meter [1,094 yards] race in a world record time of 3:12:00.

1928

Women compete in five track and field events in the Olympics. But after running the 800-meter [875 yards] final on a humid day, many competitors collapse from exhaustion. The all-male Olympic committee decides to drop the event.

1960

The longest distance that women run in the Rome Olympics is the 800-meter [875 yards] race.

1971

The Boston Marathon is officially opened to women. Eight finish the race. Women also run in the New York City Marathon, but it is a separate event from the men's race.

1975

Jacqueline Hansen is the first woman to run a marathon in under 2:40 with a time of 2:38:19.

1978

Grete Waitz sets a new world best of 2:32:30 in the New York City Marathon.

1984

Joan Benoit wins the first women's marathon of the modern Olympic Games with a time of 2:24:52.

1988

The women's 10,000-meter [10,936 yards] race is added to the Seoul Olympics.

The Expert Says…

" Joanie's greatest quality was always her mental toughness … The night of her surgery … she was sitting in bed almost in a fetal position. But she looked up at me and said, 'Can I start running tomorrow?' "

— Bob Sevene, Joan Benoit's coach

Think back to a time when you were determined to succeed against all odds. What motivated you to push yourself?

Take Note

This sporting event ranks #9. Women were running in an Olympic marathon for the first time. In a highly anticipated showdown between two top runners, Benoit the underdog turned in a superhuman performance to win the gold medal.
• What do you think Benoit, Waitz, and the other female runners proved to the world by this race?

5 4 3 2 1

Geoff Ogilvy hits a shot out of a bunker during the third round of the 2006 U.S. Open Championship.

VS. THE PLAYERS

SPORT: Golf

WHEN: June 1974 and 2006 — U.S. Open Championship at Winged Foot Golf Club in Mamaroneck, New York

THE SHOWDOWN: The world's greatest male golfers are pitted against a mighty course.

For those who play golf, it's not just a sport. It's an obsession. To these athletes, there is nothing more exciting than hitting the ball a few hundred yards and then watching it crawl toward the pin. At the other extreme, there is nothing more frustrating than watching that same ball skip 20 yards into a nearby bunker. A great player can look incredibly ordinary or incredibly skilled — all depending on the day. This is because anyone can swing a club, but only true masters can overcome all obstacles to win a competition.

The U.S. Open Championship takes place every June. It is a four-day tournament that always ends on Father's Day. Unlike most other golf tournaments, it is played on a different course every year. Fans looked forward to the excitement when they sat down to watch the 1974 U.S. Open at the Winged Foot Golf Club. History repeated itself in 2006, when the world's greatest male players challenged this tough course yet again. Three decades separated these tournaments, but the outcome was the same. The players faced an opponent they simply couldn't overcome — the golf course itself!

pin: *flagpole used to mark a hole's position on the green*
bunker: *hazard and/or sand trap on the course*

WINGED FOOT VS. THE PLAYERS

PLAYERS

Both tournaments at Winged Foot featured the game's golfing elite. In 1974, there were Arnold Palmer, Jack Nicklaus, Tom Watson, and Hale Irwin.

Thirty-two years later, the lineup was just as talented and included Tiger Woods, Vijay Singh, Phil Mickelson, Mike Weir, and Jim Furyk. Winged Foot has two different courses. That year, no one could beat Winged Foot's West Course. The length of the course, the length of the rough, and the firmness and speed of the greens were all carefully designed to give the players more than they could handle.

rough: *longer grass lining the fairway that is more difficult to hit from*

Hale Irwin in 1974, with his trophy after winning the U.S. Open Championship title with a score of 287

PLAY-BY-PLAY

The players knew Winged Foot was going to be tough in 1974, but they did not expect the golf course to destroy their game. Hale Irwin, the tournament winner, could only manage a score of seven over par.

In 2006, the players thought they would have the upper hand the second time around. But the final holes destroyed even the leading players in the tournament. Australian golfer Geoff Ogilvy won the tournament with a score of five over par. This meant he scored five strokes over the number of strokes set as a standard for Winged Foot.

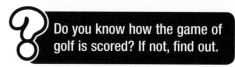 Do you know how the game of golf is scored? If not, find out.

IMPACT

The competitors had such a hard time at the 1974 U.S. Open that it quickly earned the nickname "Massacre at Winged Foot." In the 2006 tournament, the course proved to be just as challenging. Players, sports commentators, golf enthusiasts, and fans all agreed on one thing — tournament players took home their prize money, but Winged Foot definitely won the showdown.

enthusiasts: *very devoted fans*

 Do you think golf is athletic enough to be considered a sport? Explain your answer.

Quick Fact
The first U.S. Open Men's Championship was played on October 4, 1895, in Newport, Rhode Island. It was a 36-hole competition that lasted only a day.

Quick Fact
What was Hale Irwin's strategy for winning? He looked at how poorly other players were doing and decided not to get worked up about his own less-than-stellar performance.

The Expert Says...
"We're not trying to humiliate the best players in the world. We're simply trying to identify who they are."

— Sandy Tatum, former USGA president and chair of the championship committee, 1974 U.S. Open

10   9   **8**   7   6

Schooling the Pros

★ ★ ★ ★ ★ ★ ★ ★ ★ ★ ★ ★ ★ ★ ★ ★ ★ ★ ★

Have you ever watched or played golf? Check out this glossary to learn more about the game.

Tiger Woods

ACE hole in one — driving the ball from the tee to the hole with just one stroke

BIRDIE one stroke under par for the hole

BOGEY one shot over par for the hole

DRIVE hitting the ball with maximum force

FAIRWAY area golfers aim for between the tee and the green

GREEN area on the course for putting and where the hole is located

HAZARD any sand trap, bunker, or water on the course

LINE correct path of a putt to the hole when putting

MARKER small object, like a coin, which is used to mark the spot of the ball when it is lifted off the putting green

PAR number of strokes set as a standard for each hole or the entire course

PUTT stroke that makes a golf ball roll into the hole on the green

RUN distance the ball rolls on the ground or when it lands on the ground

STANCE position of a player's feet when preparing to hit the ball

TEE device, usually a wooden peg, that the ball is placed on for hitting

? What do you think would make a golf course challenging for even the game's greatest players?

Mike Weir

Take Note

This showdown swings in at #8. Instead of competing against one another, the golfers were being challenged by the golf course. Many of golf's superstars were humbled by Winged Foot, a golf course that proved to be a formidable opponent!

• What are the pros and cons of making a golf course especially difficult for golfers? Do you think it's a good idea? Why or why not?

5   4   3   2   1

7 ARGENTINA

Argentina's Gabriel Heinze (right) and Brazil's Robinho (left) battle for the ball in the first half of their soccer World Cup qualifying match in Buenos Aires, June 8, 2005.

ARGENTINA VS. BRAZIL–© SANTIAGO PANDOLFI/REUTERS/CORBIS

VS. BRAZIL

SPORT: Soccer

WHEN: Every soccer match between the two teams from 1920 until today

THE SHOWDOWN: A long-standing rivalry between Argentina and Brazil — two of the world's soccer powerhouses

When it comes to rivalries, you won't find one as intense as the decades-old soccer showdown between Brazil and Argentina. To say these two teams dislike each other is an understatement. Their feud sprang from political reasons, but these days few people remember the events that sparked this conflict. They can only think of the matches, victories, and goals. A men's soccer match between these archrivals is one that neither side wants to lose. Sometimes it is even more important than winning the actual championship.

What makes these two teams so incredible is their ability to consistently perform at peak level. And with bragging rights to some of the best players in soccer history, their face offs are guaranteed to be intense. You will sometimes hear fans call into a radio show and talk about how much they "love" one particular team and "hate" the other. This certainly might be true. But when it comes to Brazil, Argentina, and the sport called the "beautiful game," the emotions involved go far beyond the soccer field ...

---

understatement: *saying something in a mild way, without emphasis*

ARGENTINA VS. BRAZIL

PLAYERS

Argentina and Brazil are world superpowers in soccer. Each has had great success in many international competitions. Between the two countries, they have won the World Cup a total of seven times. A long-debated question fuels this historic showdown: Who is the greatest player in the history of soccer? Is it Pelé from Brazil or Maradona from Argentina?

World Cup: *international soccer competition that takes place every four years*

Quick Fact

Over the course of his career, superstar Pelé had many offers to play in Europe, including a million-dollar bid from Italy. These offers led Brazilian President Janio Quadros to declare Pelé a "national treasure" so he couldn't leave Brazil to play for other countries.

? In an international match, would you only cheer for your country's team? Why or why not? Explain.

Quick Fact

How can you tell if you're watching a showdown between Argentina and Brazil? Look for the golden shirts lined with green of the Brazilians and the blue and white vertical stripes of the Argentinians.

PLAY-BY-PLAY

Every time Argentina and Brazil compete, they are fixed on one thing — winning the match. Brazil has taken five World Cup victories to Argentina's two. Argentina has won Olympic gold, while Brazil's best has only been silver. The competition continues between these two closely matched teams.

IMPACT

Soccer is considered the world's most international sport, with devoted fans in almost every country. So much has happened between Argentina and Brazil on the soccer field that their rivalry has become a legend. They have battled each other for nearly a century and have produced some of the most beautiful, most controversial, and most fascinating games.

Brazillian supporters on their way to a World Cup match

The Expert Says...

" My mother says I was the better player and Pelé's mother says it was him. "

— Diego Maradona, legendary Argentinian soccer player

Who Is Better?

Both countries have laid claim to the greatest soccer player of all time. Is it Pelé from Brazil or Maradona from Argentina? This chart compares the two players.

	MARADONA	PELÉ
Nickname:	Pibe de Oro (Golden Boy)	O Rei (The King)
Strength:	His short height and strong legs gave him an advantage in short sprints. He used strategy, was a team player, and was very technical with the ball. He could manage himself well in small areas, and would attract defenders only to quickly dash away or pass the ball to an open teammate.	Often considered the complete midfield and attacking player, he was completely two-footed (having equal control of the ball with either foot), a successful scorer, exceptional at dribbling and passing the ball, and was a remarkably good tackler. He was also known for his speed and kicking strength.
Signature Move:	One of his trademark moves was the "Rabona." This is like a behind-the-back pass in basketball, only with the feet. The player puts his weight on one leg and crosses his other leg to the outside to strike the ball. He was also a dangerous free kicker.	His most spectacular signature move was probably the "bicycle kick." This move is done by throwing the body up into the air, making a scissor movement with the legs to get one leg high overhead to reach the ball, which gets kicked backward over the head.
Greatest Goal:	Argentina was playing England in the 1986 World Cup. Maradona ran from his own half, beating every English player who stood in his way and finished it off past the helpless goalie Peter Shilton.	Brazil was playing against Sweden in the 1958 World Cup. Pelé flicked the ball over a Swedish defender and then hit it home from close range.
Crowning Achievement:	Throughout his professional career he played 692 official games and scored 352 goals. He played 90 games for the Argentine National Team and scored 33 goals, eight of them in World Cups.	He scored over 1,200 career goals — beating other professional soccer players by leaps and bounds. But more importantly, he won three World Cups!

Take Note

The rivalry between Argentina and Brazil is so heated partly because there have been so many incidents that ended with injuries, accusations of unfairness, and even cheating. The intensity of this long-standing rivalry places this showdown at #7 on our list.

• Do you think the intense rivalry between these two teams takes away the spirit of the sport? Why or why not?

5   4   3   2   1

Larry Bird of the Boston Celtics poses with Magic Johnson of the Los Angeles Lakers in 1983.

SPORT: Basketball

WHEN: Beginning with the NCAA Championship Game in 1979 and ending with the 1987 NBA Finals

THE SHOWDOWN: The long-standing rivalry between Larry Bird, who played for the Boston Celtics, and Earvin "Magic" Johnson, who led the Los Angeles Lakers

When it comes to hardwood drama, few would argue that the greatest rivalry in basketball was between Larry Bird, the 6'9" small forward, and Magic Johnson, the 6'9" point guard. These two players first battled each other in college when Bird's Indiana State Sycamores met Johnson's Michigan State Spartans for the 1979 National Collegiate Athletic Association (NCAA) Championship. Bird came away with top honors as the best player in college that year, but Johnson and his Spartans claimed the title.

But this was only the beginning. Both entered the National Basketball Association (NBA) for the 1979–1980 season. Bird and Johnson kick-started careers in which each won multiple Most Valuable Player (MVP) awards, made numerous All-Star appearances, and competed in dozens of NBA Championships. They put up numbers that most other NBA superstars could only dream of. Their on-court showdowns in the 1980s not only defined the game for a decade, but raised expectations about the level of play that both fans and critics could expect from top players.

---

small forward: *smaller than a power forward whose play is characterized by quickness and scoring ability*

point guard: *guard who is mainly responsible for running the offense*

JOHNSON VS. BIRD

PLAYERS

Bird was a small-town kid who grew up in French Lick, Indiana. Earvin Johnson grew up in Lansing, Michigan. He got his nickname "Magic" from a reporter who saw him play a game in high school and was impressed by his amazing passing. When Bird joined the Boston Celtics for the 1979–1980 season, the team won 32 more games than the season before. Johnson joined the Los Angeles Lakers that same year and his team improved by 23 wins.

PLAY-BY-PLAY

Everyone expected fireworks whenever Bird and Johnson went head-to-head. Each time they met in the NBA Finals, it was guaranteed entertainment. The fans couldn't get enough. Thanks to the way these superstars elevated their teams, the championship matchups just kept adding up. Johnson ended his career with five NBA titles. He was also league MVP three times. Bird won three championships and racked up three MVP awards.

IMPACT

No other basketball rivalry measures up to what is now recognized as the most amazing decade-long showdown in the sport's history. Not only did these two amazing players raise the status of their teams, but they raised the profile of the entire league, moving it into the spotlight. The 1984 NBA Finals featuring Johnson and Bird were arguably the most-watched telecasts ever.

? The Boston Celtics and Los Angeles Lakers had a rivalry long before Bird and Johnson joined their teams. How do you think the historic rivalry between these teams added to the intensity of the showdown between Bird and Johnson?

The Expert Says...

" Of all the people I play against, the only one I truly fear is Larry Bird. "

— Magic Johnson

Bird and Johnson compete for a rebound at the Great Western Forum in 1986.

Quick Fact

Johnson and Bird were both easy choices for the Basketball Hall of Fame. Bird was added in 1998, while Johnson was voted in four years later, in 2002.

? What qualities or skills do you think a great basketball player should have to be added to the Basketball Hall of Fame?

Quick Fact

Bird and Johnson were great individual as well as team players. Bird was known for being a clutch performer. He broke opponents' hearts with his deadly passing and shooting. Magic was one of the purest passers in NBA history. Always dribbling at top speed, he left his opponents in the dust with his no-look assists and long bounce passes.

JOHNSON VS. BIRD

An NBA Championship Trilogy

Magic Johnson and Larry Bird met three times in the NBA Finals. Check out this timeline to get the play-by-play.

1984
THE BIRD TAKES FLIGHT

This first NBA Finals confrontation showed brilliant effort by both players, including an MVP performance from Bird. The series went the full seven games. The Boston Celtics won games two and four in overtime to even out the series twice (talk about suspense!). Bird was outstanding, averaging just over 27 points and 14 rebounds a game.

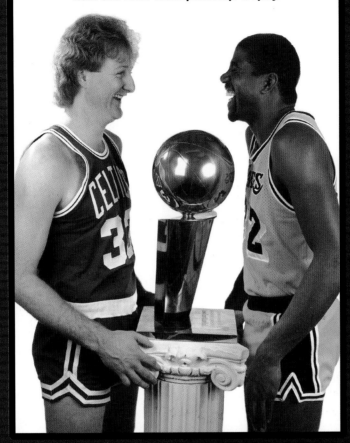

Bird and Johnson pose for a portrait with the NBA Championship Trophy.

1985
ENTER SHOWTIME!

Game one was known as the Memorial Day Massacre for the Los Angeles Lakers. Magic walked off the court with only one rebound and a humiliating 148 – 114 defeat. Bird responded by slumping in games two and three. By game four, the series was all tied up at two games apiece. In the fifth game, Johnson and Kareem Abdul-Jabbar took over, sinking some key baskets to seal the deal. The Lakers finally beat their nemesis!

nemesis: *long-standing rival*

1987 SHOW ME THE MAGIC!

It looked like Johnson and the Los Angeles Lakers were unstoppable, jumping out with an impressive 2 – 0 series lead. The Boston Celtics managed to win game three, but the next game proved pivotal. With two seconds left in the game and the Lakers down 106 – 105, Johnson pulled off a baby sky-hook, arching the ball over his defender and into the basket to win the game by a single point.

sky-hook: *hook shot invented by Kareem Abdul-Jabbar*

Take Note

Bird and Johnson's 10-year-long rivalry makes its way to the #6 spot. It breathed life back into a fading NBA. It was one of the greatest showdowns between individual players in any amateur or professional team sport.

• Think of another long-standing rivalry or showdown between two individual players in a sport. How was this rivalry important to the development of the sport?

5 4 3 2 1

Quarterback Joe Namath of the New York Jets fades back to pass against the Baltimore Colts during Super Bowl III.

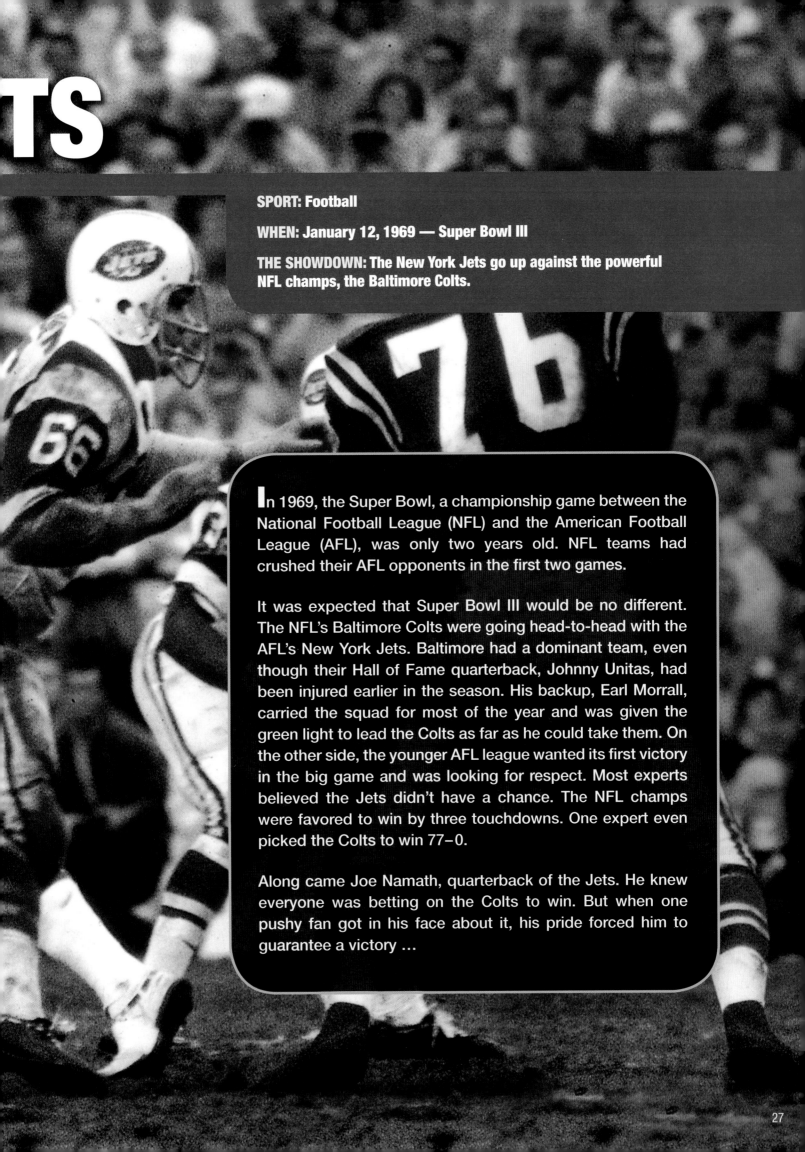

TS

SPORT: Football

WHEN: January 12, 1969 — Super Bowl III

THE SHOWDOWN: The New York Jets go up against the powerful NFL champs, the Baltimore Colts.

In 1969, the Super Bowl, a championship game between the National Football League (NFL) and the American Football League (AFL), was only two years old. NFL teams had crushed their AFL opponents in the first two games.

It was expected that Super Bowl III would be no different. The NFL's Baltimore Colts were going head-to-head with the AFL's New York Jets. Baltimore had a dominant team, even though their Hall of Fame quarterback, Johnny Unitas, had been injured earlier in the season. His backup, Earl Morrall, carried the squad for most of the year and was given the green light to lead the Colts as far as he could take them. On the other side, the younger AFL league wanted its first victory in the big game and was looking for respect. Most experts believed the Jets didn't have a chance. The NFL champs were favored to win by three touchdowns. One expert even picked the Colts to win 77–0.

Along came Joe Namath, quarterback of the Jets. He knew everyone was betting on the Colts to win. But when one pushy fan got in his face about it, his pride forced him to guarantee a victory …

JETS VS. COLTS

PLAYERS

The Baltimore Colts had two talented quarter-backs, Johnny Unitas and Earl Morrall, a great receiving corps, and a defensive team led by legendary lineman Bubba Smith. The New York Jets were also a strong squad. They had Joe Namath leading the way and future Hall of Famer Don Maynard receiving. But player for player, the Jets didn't appear to match up well against the Colts.

PLAY-BY-PLAY

There likely wouldn't have been much hype for what was expected to be a lopsided game. But Namath created hype by publicly guaranteeing a victory for the Jets. If the Jets lost, Namath would spend the rest of his career living down his claim. But what if they won?

Namath controlled the game by reading the Colts' defense. The Jets won the Super Bowl with a final score of 16–7 and Namath, without throwing a single touchdown pass, was named the MVP.

IMPACT

Namath's guarantee made Super Bowl III one of the greatest sports showdowns of all time. The image of the confident Namath leading his underestimated team to victory on the field, then waving his finger in a "we're number one" salute, is more than just a cherished piece of football legend. This victory also gave the AFL more credit, which led to a merger between the two leagues.

Baltimore Colts quarterback Johnny Unitas

? The Jets were not expected to win because they were an AFL team — at the time this league was considered weaker than the NFL. When watching sporting events, do you root for the more popular team or the underdog? Explain why.

The Expert Says...

"We sent a message to all the underdogs out there. If you want something bad enough and you aren't afraid to lay it on the line, you can do it.

— Joe Namath

Quick Fact

Even though they lost to the Jets, the Colts were still a great team. Two years later in 1971, they won Super Bowl V against the Dallas Cowboys.

10   **9**   **8**   **7**   **6**

HE GUARANTEED IT

By Ray Didinger

THIS ARTICLE EXPLAINS HOW JOE NAMATH CREATED HYPE FOR SUPER BOWL III.

On Thursday night before the game, Namath was honored by the Miami Touchdown Club as its player of the year. As he stepped to the microphone, a voice in the crowd — belonging to a Colts' fan, obviously — called out: "Hey, Namath, we're going to kick your butt."...

"I said, 'Whoa, wait a minute. You guys have been talking for two weeks now' — meaning the Colts' fans and the media — 'and I'm tired of hearing it,'" Namath remembers. "I said, 'I've got news for you. We're gonna win the game. I guarantee it.'" ...

It was not until he sat down that Namath realized what he had done. He had guaranteed a victory. Surely, this would be the lead story in every newspaper and on every television sports show in the country. ...

Jets' coach Weeb Ewbank knew nothing of Namath's comments until the next day when he awoke to find the "guarantee" bannered across the front page of the morning paper. ...

"I asked Joe what possessed him to do such a thing," Ewbank said. "I said, 'Don't you know Shula will use this to fire up his team?' Joe said, 'Coach, if they need press clippings to get ready, they're in trouble.'"

"[B]ut Joe always had a way of delivering. He didn't mind pressure. It seemed to make him play better. I figured if he said it, he would just have to back it up."

— www.profootballhof.com

? Because of Namath's guarantee, the AFL's reputation as a league rested heavily on the Jets' victory over the Colts in Super Bowl III. Do you think this was fair to the other AFL teams and players. Why or why not?

Take Note

At #5, Super Bowl III is the greatest showdown between a favored team and an underdog. Namath's guarantee put more pressure on himself and his team — the difference is they delivered! Namath staked his entire career on one game, and amazingly won!
• Do you think guaranteeing victory was a good way for Namath to motivate his team or do you think it added too much pressure? Explain your answer.

Joe Namath

5   4   3

29

Bobby Riggs and Billie Jean King arm-wrestle at a press conference, where they announce they'll face each other in a $100,000 winner-take-all tennis match.

NG

SPORT: Tennis

WHEN: September 20, 1973, Houston Astrodome

THE SHOWDOWN: Twenty-nine-year-old tennis star Billie Jean King is challenged by 55-year-old former tennis champion Bobby Riggs.

It was 1973 and the women's liberation movement was at its peak. Billie Jean King was one of the greatest female tennis players the world had ever seen. She had already won grand slams in singles and mixed doubles, achieved an impressive number of tournament victories, and won the distinction of having previously been ranked the number one female tennis player in the world. Almost twice King's age, Bobby Riggs was the outspoken former tennis prodigy, Wimbledon champion, and men's number one player.

Riggs claimed that when it came to competition, women simply couldn't match up. He thought he had already proven his point by beating the world's top female player, Margaret Court, in an exhibition match. Now, he was willing to go one step further and take on the fiercely determined Billie Jean King. It would go down as one of the greatest sports showdowns in history.

grand slams: *winning Wimbledon along with the Australian, French, and U.S. Opens*
prodigy: *unusually gifted person*

RIGGS VS. KING

PLAYERS

King's accomplishments were second to none on the tennis court. She was one of the top female tennis players of her era and would eventually end her career with 20 Wimbledon titles. Riggs, on the other hand, hadn't been at the top of his game since 1947. He had only recently returned to the public arena to challenge the sport's top female players.

PLAY-BY-PLAY

Male chauvinists thought Riggs would show the world that women simply couldn't compete with men, but feminists were certain King could prove them wrong. In a stadium packed with over 30,000 people and watched by over 40 million on prime-time television, this event turned out to be the most watched tennis match in history. It soon became obvious who was the stronger player. King ran Riggs all over the place, blowing him off the court in a 6 – 4, 6 – 3, 6 – 3, straight sets victory.

IMPACT

In front of an audience of millions, King proved the ability of female athletes. Her performance paved the way for the equal treatment of women in sports and inspired an entire generation of women to believe in themselves.

male chauvinists: *men who believe that women are inferior*

Billie Jean King entered the Astrodome on a red velvet throne carried by football players dressed in togas.

Bobby Riggs was brought into the stadium on a carriage pulled by young women.

Quick Fact

Despite their big showdown, Billie Jean King and Bobby Riggs were not enemies. They had a friendly relationship with each other, right up until Riggs's death from cancer in 1995.

The Expert Says...

" I thought it would set us back 50 years if I didn't win that match. It would ruin the women's tour and affect all women's self-esteem. "

— Billie Jean King

Have you ever had to compete against someone you considered a friend? Why do you think it's important for people to be able to compete while still staying friends?

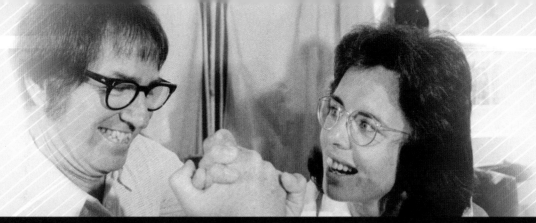

The BATTLE of the SEXES
= The Beginnings of "Hype"

This report explains how Bobby Riggs used the media to bring attention to this larger-than-life match.

Because this match took place in 1973, it was years ahead of its time. It created "hype" — the extreme publicity we often see before important political, social, and athletic events today.

Riggs was a master of hype. He gained a reputation for challenging unsuspecting players and taking strange odds in the process. In his earlier battle with Margaret Court, Riggs gave her a large bouquet of roses right before the match to throw her off balance. In some earlier matches, he even used a frying pan instead of a racquet.

The "Battle of the Sexes" saw more hype than any other sporting event of the time. Not only did Riggs land himself on the cover of *Sports Illustrated*, but he announced to the media many times that he wanted to beat King in the match. He got people's attention by announcing that if he was going to be called a male chauvinist pig, he wanted to be "the number one pig."

Adding to the spectacle was legendary broadcaster Howard Cosell calling the match, along with famous personalities like heavyweight boxer George Foreman and pro footballer Jim Brown acting as security.

Even though King worked at training hard and kept out of the limelight, Riggs did whatever he could to push her front and center. This showed the public how difficult it was for well-known personalities to stay out of the media spotlight. The Battle of the Sexes taught us that hype is not something one person can stop, especially if someone else is determined to create it.

Quick Fact

Before the match, Riggs made many television and radio appearances to try to psych out King. She, on the other hand, played it cool and kept a low profile to get under his skin.

? Compare the pre-game tactics of both Riggs and King. If you were preparing for an important match, which strategy would you use and why?

Take Note

Our #4 choice, the Battle of the Sexes was not just an overblown tennis match — it helped to advance the women's liberation movement by leaps and bounds. King's victory proved once and for all that women could compete with, and firmly crush, their male competitors.
- Can you think of any other time when men and women challenged one another in sports? How do you think King's victory back in 1973 helped to influence society's attitudes toward women in sports today?

5   **4**   3   2   1

Mickey Mantle (left) and Roger Maris (right)

SPORT: Baseball

WHEN: 1961 Major League Baseball season

THE SHOWDOWN: Roger Maris and Mickey Mantle race to break Babe Ruth's single-season home run record.

Roger Maris didn't play baseball to win popularity contests. He was traded by the Kansas City Athletics to the New York Yankees before the start of the 1960 season and quickly made an impression on New York fans — but it wasn't a good one. He didn't try to win over the media so he faced a lot of criticism from the press.

Mickey Mantle was not always the most popular Yankee either, because he replaced the popular Joe DiMaggio in the early 1950s. But he proved himself by being a key part of several championship Yankee teams. He became one of their greatest power hitters. His stats were legendary.

The 1961 Major League Baseball season would be a special year as both Maris and Mantle chased Babe Ruth's 60 home run mark. To fans, the Babe's 1927 record stood for baseball perfection and many thought his record could never be beaten. But if anyone was going to do it, fans wanted it to be Mantle, not Maris. Anybody but Maris ...

MARIS VS. MANTLE

PLAYERS

Maris had played in New York for only a short time, but he made an impact with his MVP award in 1960. Still, critics felt he was missing the charm they admired in other ballplayers. Mantle had been a Yankee since the early 1950s. Although he had a rocky start to his career, New York fans grew to love him.

PLAY-BY-PLAY

As the summer of 1961 passed, everyone realized that both Maris and Mantle had a shot at breaking Babe Ruth's 60 home run record. Fans cheered Mantle, but hissed and booed Maris. And since the league added eight games to the schedule that year, many questioned whether a new record should even count. The players battled each other until Mantle was sidelined with a leg infection late in the season. He ended up with 54 "dingers." This was still six short of Ruth's mark. Maris went on to hit his 61st homer in the last game of the season to break the Babe's 34-year-old record.

IMPACT

The race to hit 61 home runs in the summer of 1961 has become one of the most important events in professional baseball. This competition did not make Maris a fan favorite in New York, but made Mantle even more popular.

The Expert Says...

"Now they talk on the radio about the record set by Ruth, and DiMaggio, and Henry Aaron. But they rarely mention mine. Do you know what I have to show for the 61 home runs? Nothing, exactly nothing."

— Roger Maris

? Both fans and the media chose sides during the home run race. How have other people's opinions ever affected your performance in a game or competition?

Mickey Mantle's (left) number seven jersey was retired by the Yankees in 1969. Roger Maris's (right) number nine wasn't retired until 1984.

Quick Fact

Part of what fueled the rivalry between Maris and Mantle was their completely opposite upbringings. Maris was the son of Croatian immigrants, while Mantle was an all-American farmboy who grew up in Oklahoma.

North Dakota Speaks Out
Let Maris Rule!

Read this article to decide for yourself.

Roger Maris's home run record in 1961 was broken by a trio of ballplayers. In 1998, Mark McGwire destroyed the record by hitting an amazing 70 home runs for the St. Louis Cardinals. He was chased by Sammy Sosa, who ended up with 66 homers. Three years later, Barry Bonds of the San Francisco Giants hit an incredible 73 home runs to pass McGwire's mark.

But in 2005, the North Dakota Senate introduced a resolution to recognize Roger Maris (a native of North Dakota) as the official home run king.

Why?

There were scandals about professional baseball players taking drugs to improve their play. These scandals cast doubt on the players who broke Maris's record. The North Dakota Senate felt that Maris's record should not be taken away by players who might have cheated to break it. According to North Dakota's senator Joel Heitkamp, "In North Dakota when we think something has been wrong, we try to make it right … and when it comes to how people have taken this record [of Maris's home run] away … that's not right."

The people of North Dakota believed in fair play. They wanted to make it clear that their guy played a clean game, the kind that farm kids like Maris played in their days. And they were proud of him!

resolution: *written agreement*

Roger Maris

Quick Fact

There was controversy about Maris's record because he played at a time when there were more games in a season than Ruth's time. An asterisk was placed next to Maris's record to point this out.

Take Note

The home run race between Maris and Mantle takes the #3 spot on our list. Two men on the same team go head-to-head for baseball's most important record. This showdown lasted a whole season and created a lot of excitement.
• Babe Ruth is a legend in baseball. Find out more about his impressive career. How do his achievements compare with another sports legend such as Tiger Woods?

 Do you agree with the North Dakota Senate's resolution? Explain your answer.

5   4   **3**   2   1

Muhammad Ali (right) punches Joe Frazier (left) in the head during the seventh round of "Thrilla in Manila" that took place in the Philippines in 1975.

ER

More than a few eyebrows were raised when a flashy boxer named Cassius Clay beat Sonny Liston for the heavyweight champion of the world title in 1964. The world was further stunned when Clay found Islam, changed his name to Muhammad Ali, and was stripped of his title for refusing to fight in the Vietnam War.

Then along came humble heavyweight Joe Frazier. He quietly punched his way to the championship title that Ali no longer held. Everyone could clearly see how different these two fighters were, but no one had any idea how many sparks would fly when they faced each other in the ring.

To say their showdown was one of the all-time greatest wouldn't be enough. Over the course of their three matches, they fought 41 out of a possible 42 rounds, delivered hundreds of devastating blows, and put each other in the hospital after dishing out damage that would have ended the careers of lesser fighters. Frazier and Ali were both warriors in the ring, but their showdown turned them into legends ...

ALI VS. FRAZIER

PLAYERS

In 1971, Frazier was the undefeated heavyweight champion of the world. Ali was the undefeated former champion who had been stripped of his title for refusing to fight in the Vietnam War. Not only did these boxers deal each other their first losses, but by the end of their third and final battle in 1975, both men were living legends.

PLAY-BY-PLAY

Ali created hype long before Joe Namath or Bobby Riggs. He was the master, annoying opponents with his pre-fight stunts. Frazier won the first bout with a 15-round decision. Critics called it the "Fight of the Century." Ali won their second scrap. This 12-round victory by unanimous decision put him in line to fight George Foreman for the title. The third bout was to settle the score. It was the legendary "Thrilla in Manila." This went to Ali when Frazier's trainer ended the fight before the start of the 15th round.

---

unanimous: *complete agreement by everyone*

IMPACT

The Ali-Frazier fights were historic battles that defined the careers of both boxers. These fights turned the two heavyweight champions into legends. Their three grueling contests set the standard for all other boxing matches. With today's overhyped sporting events and extreme media coverage, fights are built with clever gimmicks and catchy taglines. The actual fight sometimes cannot match the buildup. What sets this rivalry apart is that it always lived up to its billing.

? How do you think the opposite personalities of Ali and Frazier helped to build up the excitement of their three showdowns?

"If you even dream of beating me you'd better wake up and apologize."
— Ali

Quick Fact

Ali later called his third and final fight with Frazier the "closest thing to dying" and finally admitted that his archrival was truly a "great, great fighter."

The Expert Says...

" Sit down, son, it's over. But no one will ever forget what you did here today. "

— Frazier's trainer Eddie Futch before he ended the Thrilla in Manila before the start of the 15th round

? Frazier lasted until the 14th round of the Thrilla in Manila. Why do you think Eddie Futch believed Frazier's performance would be remembered even though he lost the match? Do you think a loser in a sport can also be considered a great player? Explain why or why not.

10   9   8   7   6

TALES OF THE TAPE
A LEGENDARY TRILOGY

Muhammad Ali and Joe Frazier fought three historic heavyweight battles in the 1970s.

Fight of the Century | March 8, 1971 | Ali-Frazier II | January 28, 1974 | Thrilla in Manila | October 1, 1975

Despite their different personalities, they were extremely well-matched opponents.
This comparison chart shows how these two legendary warriors stack up ...

MUHAMMAD ALI

Birth name Cassius Marcellus Clay Jr.

Birthdate January 17, 1942

Birthplace Louisville, Kentucky

Nickname The Greatest

Weight 205 lb.

Height 6'3"

Reach 81 in.

Total fights 61

Wins 56

Wins by knockout 37

Losses 5

Draws 0

Style The key to his success was his speed. He had lightning-fast hands and a left jab that could control a fight. He also had enough agility and footwork to escape danger.

JOE FRAZIER

Birth name Joseph William Frazier

Birthdate January 12, 1944

Birthplace Beaufort, South Carolina

Nickname Smokin' Joe

Weight 210.5 lb.

Height 5'11"

Reach 73 in.

Total Fights 37

Wins 32

Wins by knockout 27

Losses 4

Draws 1

Style Frazier's best punch was a devastating left hook, but his greatest asset was his strong will. He won fights by slowly wearing down his opponents.

Quick Fact

In 1990, Muhammad Ali and Joe Frazier were both added to the International Boxing Hall of Fame.

Take Note

The rivalry between Ali and Frazier takes the #2 spot on our list. Three legendary fights with a two-to-one victory determined the greatest heavyweight boxer in history — it doesn't get much better than this.

• Research the different personalities of Ali and Frazier. How did each man reflect his personality through boxing?

5   4   3   **2**   1

U.S. hockey player John Harrington reacts after the puck was fired into the net for a goal past Soviet goalkeeper Vladimir Myshkin.

ES VS. USSR

SPORT: Men's Olympic Ice Hockey

WHEN: February 22, 1980, Lake Placid, New York

THE SHOWDOWN: The underestimated American team takes on a powerhouse Soviet squad.

Almost any American who is old enough can tell you exactly what he or she was doing on February 22, 1980. This was when Team USA scored the winning goal in the last few minutes of their legendary Olympic game against the Soviet Union. That moment triggered a spontaneous national celebration.

Made up of mostly college students and National Hockey League (NHL) hopefuls, the American team was going into this face-off as the clear underdog. Against such incredible odds, the underestimated Americans beat the legendary Soviet squad in a game that has now been dubbed the "Miracle on Ice."

It may just be the single most unforgettable moment in all of American sports history. National pride was at stake, but it was even bigger than this. Two different ways of life were competing against each other. The game was tied with less than 10 minutes to go. Then something surprising happened that would lift the pride of a nation.

UNITED STATES VS. USSR

PLAYERS

The Soviets were elite amateurs playing hockey full-time in their native country. Team USA featured the country's best college players mixed with some NHL hopefuls. American hockey newcomers like Mike Eruzione, Mark Johnson, and Ken Morrow took on some of the greatest players in Soviet ice hockey including Alexander Maltsev, Vladimir Petrov, and their legendary goalie, Vladislav Tretiak.

elite: *select few who are the best*

Quick Fact

Eruzione's goal was imprinted in the minds of Americans as "The Goal" of American hockey history, but player Mark Johnson was the team's top scorer. Teammates compared him to basketball superstar "Magic" Johnson because he was so slick with the puck.

Team USA celebrating their legendary victory just moments after the end of the game

Quick Fact

Many people mistakenly believe that Team USA beat the Soviets in the gold medal game. After they beat the Soviets, USA went on to play Finland for the gold medal. They beat Finland 4–2 to finally take the gold!

PLAY-BY-PLAY

The Soviet team started off strong against the Americans, but Team USA kept up the pace. American goalie Jim Craig was looking sharp. This helped the team build their confidence. At the end of the first period, the teams were tied 2–2. But the Soviets scored on a power play and were leading 3–2 by the end of the second period. With 8:39 left in the final period, Johnson scored again to tie the game for the U.S. Only a few minutes later, Eruzione fired a shot past Soviet goalie Vladimir Myshkin, who had replaced Tretiak at the end of the first period, to give Team USA a 4–3 lead. Craig withstood a last barrage of shots as the crowd began to count down the last few seconds of the game.

IMPACT

No other Olympic performance has touched the American people with quite the same intensity. People united to celebrate this amazing victory. The country was overcome with patriotism. In conquering what was considered the world's top hockey team, America felt it was back in control as a strong political power. The Soviets couldn't believe they had lost. Their loss of the gold medal had taken the pride out of their other Olympic triumphs that year.

power play: *attack by a team at full strength against the opposing team playing one or two players short because of a penalty*

barrage: *rapid series*

? What do you think contributed to the victory of this young American team playing against a Soviet team with so many hockey legends on their roster?

The Expert Says...

" It's the most transcending moment in the history of our sport in this country …"

— Dave Ogrean, former executive director of USA Hockey

transcending: *rising above; going beyond*

LIFE AFTER THE MIRACLE

Of the 20 players on Team USA, 13 went on to play in the NHL. Five of them would go on to play over 500 NHL games. This list details their careers as pros.

NEAL BROTEN — Appeared in 1,099 NHL games over 17 seasons, mostly with the Minnesota North Stars/Dallas Stars. A two-time All-Star, he tallied 923 career points (289 goals, 634 assists) and won a Stanley Cup as a member of the New Jersey Devils in 1994–1995.

KEN MORROW — Won a Stanley Cup in 1980 as a member of the New York Islanders. He became the first hockey player to win an Olympic gold medal and Cup in the same year. He went on to play 550 NHL games and win three more Cups, all with the Islanders.

MIKE RAMSEY — Had the longest NHL career. He played in 1,070 games over 18 years. Fourteen of those years were spent with the Buffalo Sabres, for whom he was a four-time NHL All-Star and served as team captain from 1990–1992.

DAVE CHRISTIAN — Played 14 years in the NHL. He spend most of his career with the Winnipeg Jets (as team captain) and Washington Capitals. He played a total of 1,009 games and ended his career with 773 points (340 goals, 443 assists). He made the All-Star team in 1991.

? What does it say about the skills of the 1980 American team that so many went on to play in the NHL?

MARK JOHNSON — Bounced around the NHL for several years before finding a home in New Jersey. He was a scoring threat wherever he went, tallying 508 career points (203 goals, 305 assists). He played a total of 669 games over 11 seasons. In 1984, Johnson was named the Hartford Whalers' Most Valuable Player.

Take Note

The Miracle on Ice took place at a time when the United States and the Soviet Union did not get along very well. There was so much at stake. Not only were two teams from different countries competing against each other, but each stood for different views, values, and political beliefs. This showdown takes the #1 prize.
• The result of this showdown was dubbed the Miracle on Ice. Do you think it is an appropriate name? Why?

5   4   3   2   1

We Thought …

Here are the criteria we used in ranking the 10 greatest sports showdowns.

The showdown:
- Had a lasting impact inside and outside the sport
- Was highly anticipated by fans and media
- Involved high stakes for the winner or loser
- Created a first in the sport
- Had an unexpected and surprising outcome
- Attracted worldwide attention
- Brought about an immediate change
- Involved a victory beyond the monetary reward
- Involved well-known competitors
- Involved rivalry, competition, and pride

What Do You Think?

1. Do you agree with our ranking? If you don't, try ranking these showdowns yourself. Justify your ranking with data from your own research and reasoning. You may refer to our criteria, or you may want to draw up your own list of criteria.

2. Here are three showdowns that we considered but in the end did not include in our top 10 list: Pittsburg Steelers vs. Dallas Cowboys, New York Yankees vs. Brooklyn Dodgers, and Seabiscuit vs. War Admiral.
   • Find out more about them. Do you think they should have made our list? Give reasons for your response.
   • Are there other showdowns that you think should have made our list? Explain your choices.

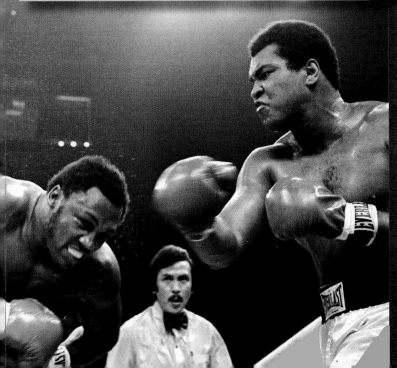

Index